Glow-in-the-Dark Animals

FIREFLIES

Sara Howell

PowerKiDS
press.

New York

Published in 2015 by The Rosen Publishing Group, Inc.
29 East 21st Street, New York, NY 10010

First Edition

Editor: Katie Kawa
Book Design: Katelyn Londino

Photo Credits: Cover James Jordan/Moment/Getty Images; cover, pp. 1–24 (background texture) olesya k/Shutterstock.com; pp. 4–5 tomosang/Moment/Getty Images; pp. 6–7 Tyler Fox/Shutterstock.com; pp. 8–9 Elliotte Rusty Harold/Shutterstock.com; p. 10 (lightbulb) Africa Studio/Shutterstock.com; pp. 10–11 (fireflies), 20–21 Steven Puetzer/Photographer's Choice/ Getty Images; p. 13 http://en.wikipedia.org/wiki/Firefly#mediaviewer/File:Leuchtk%C3%A4fer_-_Firefly.JPG; pp. 14–15 Fer Gregory/Shutterstock.com; pp. 16–17 Medford Taylor/National Geographic/Getty Images; pp. 18–19 Paul A. Zahl/National Geographic/Getty Images; p. 22 Brandon Alms/Shutterstock.com.

Library of Congress Cataloging-in-Publication Data

Howell, Sara, author.
 Fireflies / Sara Howell.
     pages cm. — (Glow-in-the-dark animals)
 Includes index.
 ISBN 978-1-4994-0117-2 (pbk.)
 ISBN 978-1-4994-0118-9 (6 pack)
 ISBN 978-1-4994-0114-1 (library binding)
 1. Fireflies—Juvenile literature. 2. Bioluminescence—Juvenile literature. I. Title.
 QL596.L28H74 2015
 595.76'44—dc23
                            2014024158

Manufactured in the United States of America

CPSIA Compliance Information: Batch #CW15PK: For Further Information contact Rosen Publishing, New York, New York at 1-800-237-9932

CONTENTS

MEET THE FIREFLY

Have you ever been outside on a warm night and seen a quick flash of light close by? If so, you may have seen an **insect** called a firefly. A firefly isn't actually a fly. It belongs to a group of insects called beetles. These insects have two sets of wings. The stiff outer wings **protect** the inner flight wings when the beetle isn't flying.

There are at least 400,000 known species, or kinds, of beetles, including ladybugs and dung beetles. However, the firefly's ability to use its body to produce light sets it apart from other beetles.

Fireflies are also known as lightning bugs.

NEWS FLASH!

There are more beetles on Earth
than any other kind of insect.

WARM AND WET HOMES

There are about 2,000 different firefly species around the world. They live mostly in warm areas. Some also live in places that are temperate, or not too hot or too cold. Fireflies commonly live where it's **humid**. However, some live in dry parts of the world. These fireflies tend to stay close to areas with standing water, such as ponds and **marshes**.

Fireflies often live in areas with tall grasses. When they're not flying, they can often be found resting on blades of tall grass. It's a good place to hide from predators.

An area of standing water surrounded by tall grass
is a good place to find fireflies.

A CLOSER LOOK

The largest fireflies can grow up to 1 inch (2.5 cm) long. Like all insects, fireflies have six legs and three main parts to their body. These parts are called the head, thorax, and abdomen. Fireflies also have a pair of antennae, or feelers, on their head.

The head is the first part of a firefly's body. The thorax is in the middle. The abdomen is the rear part of the body. A firefly's light **organ** can be found at the end of its abdomen.

It's often hard to tell one species of firefly from another. It's also hard to tell male and female fireflies apart when they aren't glowing. One of the best ways to tell males and females apart is to look at the organ that produces the firefly's light. Males and females have different-looking light organs.

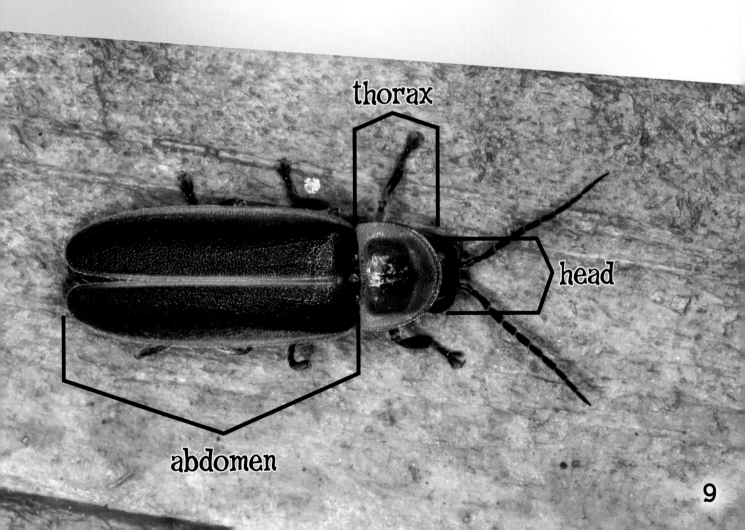

thorax

head

abdomen

FIREFLY FLASHES

A firefly's ability to produce light with its body is called bioluminescence (by-oh-loo-muh-NEH-suhns). Most fireflies produce a greenish-yellow light. This light is seen in flashes. The length of the flashes and the time between flashes depends on the firefly species.

The organ that creates a firefly's glow is called the lantern. It takes in **oxygen** from the air. The oxygen mixes with a **chemical** in the lantern to create light. This light is called cold light because it doesn't give off any heat.

A glowing lightbulb gives off both light and heat. A glowing firefly only gives off light.

NEWS FLASH!

Other bioluminescent animals
include certain species of shrimp,
jellyfish, and snails.

MATING SEASON

Fireflies glow to **attract** a mate, or another firefly to make babies with. To attract a mate, male fireflies fly around an area and flash in a certain pattern. Females of the same species recognize this pattern. If they're interested in mating with the males, they flash back. Males with longer and brighter flashes often attract the most females.

Once a male and female have mated, the female lays her eggs in wet soil. Larvae **hatch** from these eggs in about three to four weeks.

Firefly larvae look like worms, but they're also bioluminescent!

NEWS FLASH!

Female fireflies don't need to fly around to attract males. They stay in one place, and the males come to them!

GREAT IMITATORS

Compared to many animals, fireflies live very short lives. Some species of fireflies spend over a year as larvae. Then, their body begins to change into the adult form. This is called the pupa stage of their life cycle. Once fireflies become adults, though, they live only a few weeks.

When a firefly flashes its light at another firefly, it's like one person talking to another person.

Adult fireflies use flashes of light to **communicate** with each other. Fireflies recognize other members of their species by their pattern of flashes. However, some species are able to imitate, or copy, the patterns of other species. This trick can scare other fireflies away or draw them close enough to be eaten by the imitator!

NEWS FLASH!

Many species of firefly larvae live underground until they become adults.

A CHANGING DIET

Firefly larvae are carnivores. This means they eat other animals. Firefly larvae eat worms, snails, and slugs. They have a special chemical that helps them catch **prey**. The chemical causes prey to lose feeling in their body. The prey is then unable to move as the larvae eat them alive.

When larvae become adult fireflies, their diet, or the food they eat, changes. Many adult fireflies feed on plant pollen and nectar. Some species eat other fireflies. Others don't appear to eat at all!

Nectar and pollen, which can be found in flowers, are common foods for fireflies.

PREDATORS AND OTHER DANGERS

A firefly's bright flashes often attract the attention of predators, such as bats, spiders, and toads. However, fireflies are able to protect themselves. When a firefly is attacked, it sheds a few drops of blood. This is called reflex bleeding. The blood has a bad taste and can be poisonous to some predators. These animals soon learn to stay away from fireflies.

Predators are not the only danger fireflies face. Fireflies live in fields, meadows, and other open spaces. As humans use more of these spaces to build homes and other buildings, fireflies lose their natural **habitat**.

This spider is about to learn that fireflies don't taste very good!

NEWS FLASH!

Some firefly species get poisonous blood from eating other species. Then, their babies are born with poisonous blood.

LIGHTING UP THE SKY

People around the world look forward to spotting fireflies on warm nights. Most fireflies rest during the day. However, their flashes can be seen clearly once it gets dark and they begin to fly around.

Some people try to capture fireflies in jars to see them glow up close. While catching fireflies can be fun, it's important to be very careful with them. It's better to watch fireflies light up in their natural habitats. This is a safer way to watch and study fireflies. Luckily for us, those natural habitats are often our own backyards!

If you ever catch fireflies in a jar, make sure you let them go when you're done looking at them.

FUN FIREFLY FACTS

1. Fireflies are nocturnal, which means they're active mostly at night. During the day, they rest on leaves or blades of grass.

2. Fireflies can't see blue light. Using a blue flashlight is the safest way to look at fireflies.

3. Not all species of fireflies glow, including some species found in the western United States.

4. Fireflies flash more quickly when it's warm. As it gets colder, the time between a firefly's flashes increases.

5. The timing of a firefly's flashes can change with the moon. On nights when the moon looks brighter, fireflies begin flashing later.

6. Fireflies have large eyes, which help them see in the dark.

7. The chemical that helps a firefly produce light is used by scientists for many purposes, including studying sickness in humans and testing for food safety.

GLOSSARY

attract: To cause to come close.

chemical: Matter that can be mixed with other matter to cause changes.

communicate: To share ideas and feelings.

habitat: The natural home for a plant or animal.

hatch: To come out of an egg.

humid: Having a lot of water in the air.

insect: A small animal that has six legs and three body parts, and commonly has wings.

marsh: An area of soft, wet land that has many grasses and other plants.

organ: A part inside the body that does a job.

oxygen: A gas that animals and people need in order to live.

prey: An animal hunted by other animals for food.

protect: To keep safe.

INDEX

WEBSITES

Due to the changing nature of Internet links, PowerKids Press has developed an online list of websites related to the subject of this book. This site is updated regularly. Please use this link to access the list: www.powerkidslinks.com/gitda/fflies